François Bucher / Josef Albers   Despite Straight Lines

Josef Albers

Despite Straight Lines

An analysis of his graphic constructions
by François Bucher
Captions by Josef Albers
New Haven and London:
Yale University Press, 1961

The statements and poems by Josef Albers
are reprinted by permission of the copyright owner,
The Readymade Press, New Haven, Connecticut

Typography by Max Caflisch
Printed by Benteli AG, Berne-Bümpliz
Blocks by Hermann Denz AG, Berne
Printed in Switzerland

Content

I   Introduction

For Heraclitus, ultimate creative force lies in motion and change which govern both the atom and cosmic movement in a balance of birth and destruction.

Today, at the beginning of a new world age, motion, process, and relativity have become basic concerns of intelligent humanity. The artist, an originator as well as a sensitive interpreter of the spiritual forces shaping history, recognizes and reflects this deep involvement and has again transformed complex philosophical and theoretical systems into images which can be understood by all who have sharpened their visual perception.

Process, relativity, and motion are essential concerns of the seemingly chaotic artistic production of our time. Most contemporary creators show us a universe in dynamic flux. But none of them has concentrated his attention on the relativity of visual phenomena as tenaciously as Josef Albers.

In the static vanishing-point system of Renaissance perspective dominant to the end of the 19th century, parallel lines met on the horizon, and made the infinite tangible for the viewer. With Mondrian they became parallels once more which could meet only outside our immediate world of experience. For the Abstract Expressionist a painting is a never-ending process. For the modern sculptor mass is not fixed. It may actually move, as in the mobiles, or else its complex texture of polished brillance or pierced material may make it elusive. Le Corbusier's Unité d'Habitation finds its echo in the mountains and the blazing plane of the Mediterranean, while Ronchamp's sweeping roof line demands contact with universal space.

This awareness of a constantly changing and ever intangible image of reality forms the paintings and especially the graphic constructions of Josef Albers, and makes him truly a contemporary, or, in other words, a man who has submitted himself to the full impact of the present.

There is no world without a stage
and no one lives for not-appearing.

Seeing of ears invites to speak,
knowing of eyes invites to show.

Notice also, silence sounds
listen to the voice of color.

Semblance proves it can be truth
as every form has sense and meaning.   J. A.

Most of the modern painters have used a perceptual approach, that is, complex shapes and colors to grip our attention, and have therefore frequently returned to a vocabulary which ties in with the western visual tradition as represented by Turner or Monet. The work of Albers, however, has remained primarily conceptual and is based upon the exploration of universal phenomena.

Art from the Renaissance onward was concerned with historical or social, with observed or imagined events. It concentrated therefore on exact observation of the immediately visible world and reached its conclusion in the paintings of the Impressionists. Thus it was an art which stressed 'out-sight'.

The expressionistic movements emphasized a personal imagery, which – unsystematically – became more and more abstract. The Cubists and Constructivists explored a plastic experience inherent in geometric forms. It is in their lineage that Albers creates. The distortions used by the Cubists introduced a time sequence with mixed success. The represented objects were fragmented. Through their color and structure they became a pictorial entity which was almost totally detached from the original subject matter. These splinters of daily life could still awaken associations foreign to the organism of the painting itself. The same is true for most of the constructivist and frequently for abstract production.

Through the exclusion of any overtones extraneous to the picture Albers wants to bring these experiments to their logical conclusion. For him our capacity to visualize the new spiritual climate around us must begin with a disciplined return to visual events which sharpen our awareness and will produce 'in-sight'.

The making of art is so complex that all of its possibilities can never be completely controlled. Consequently in his graphic constructions Albers has for more than a decade limited himself to one single element: *the line*. But even the line can expand, contract, twist, and curl. It offers temptations to which an artist can succumb and which he will rarely be able to master in an absolute way. Albers thus chose the austerity of the *straight line in relation to itself*. Through this self-imposed discipline, with its limitations and occasional frustrations, he has been able to achieve control.

Although the line constructions are almost naively intellectual and conventionally placed upon a geometric grid, they seem to assume a life of their own. They may at first tease only the eye, then occupy the mind. Finally they can suddenly attack our innermost pattern of experience. Thus the brain lacks an explanation for the phenomena straight lines can produce. Irritation, wonder, discovery, and pleasure result.

Through this extreme and conscious limitation which initially seems to evoke the obvious, or the decorative, Albers plunges us into the shocking recognition that the combination of the simplest, most basic tool of visual formulation – the straight line – contains the most illogical possibilities and is infinitely rich in visual performance. Thus Albers' art which at first seems purely conceptual partakes of the irrational and in essence searches for the absolute.

In the following pages we will deliberately try to isolate elements used by Albers to create his diagram of reality. This artificial emphasis on components will in the end help toward a fuller understanding of the inner cohesion within his 'constructed' work.

1. Synopsis

As the term 'tectonic' implies, the abstract compositions shown here are constructed, being built with elements that are produced by mechanical means and arranged in an emphasized mechanical order.

It is obvious that these constructions have no modulations (gradual increase and decrease of plastic activity) within individual lines, though graphic art ordinarily employs such modulations, and which I use, for instance, in making dry-points.

Therefore, these lithographs do not emphasize the graphic characteristics of lithographs.

I choose the zinc-litho process as the most appropriate way of achieving both the directness and precision of lines and the exact proportions of black and white, that I had developed in preparatory studies.

Although there is no actual modulation in the lines themselves, there is an illusionary modulation of volume and space which results in plastic movement.

This illusionary modulation is produced by groups of equally thick lines and is achieved through their light-dark relationships and their constellation.

These results require the use of ruler and drafting pen and establish unmodulated line as a legitimate artistic means.

In this way they oppose a belief that the handmade is better than the machine-made, or that mechanical construction is anti-graphic or unable to arouse emotion.

In this age of industrial evolution both methods have their merits.

J. A.

2. Syntax

These lithographs are built exclusively of horizontal and vertical lines which are the most two-dimensional and therefore the most non-spatial graphic elements.

These abstract compositions perform space and volume illusions of multiple images, thereby inducing several interpretations.

Receding directions are imaginary, appearing only through related junctions of horizontals and verticals.

Movements are not confined to one direction only, but interchange. Thus solid volume shifts to open space and open space to volume. Masses moving at first to one side may suddenly appear to be moving to the opposite side or in another direction.

Likewise, upward acts also as downward, forward as backward, and verticals function as horizontals. Parallels, horizontals or verticals, produce sloping planes, empty spaces become solid. Black lines produce gray tones and, for sensitive eyes, even color.

Thus we cannot remain in a single viewpoint, we need more for the sake of free vision.

1942   J. A.

*Presented are 2 stair-like figures, a large one at right,
a small one at upper left. They consist of 3, or 2½, steps
built of vertical and horizontal planes which appear
translucent or transparent.*

*The large figure, normally, is seen first and read upward,
because its lower step is largest. It also overlaps both
the connected horizontal plane (seen from underneath)
and the front of the second step which is equally related
to the following, the third step.*

*Therefore, the upward reading of the large figure
repeats 3 times a moving up, followed by a
backward down.   J. A.*

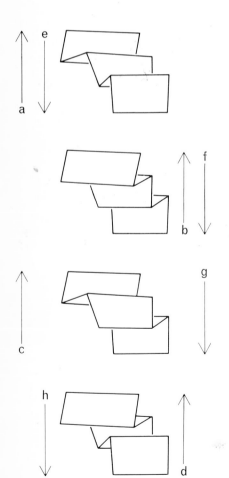

In contrast, the movement of the small figure is very ambiguous:

*(a) Receding – as in large figure: up–back, up–back, up.
     For an easy visualization, follow zig-zag edge at left.*
*(b) Advancing – the opposite of (a): up–forward, up–forward, up.
     See zig-zag edge at right.*
(c) First alternation of (a) and (b): only second step receding.
(d) Second alternation of (b) and (a): only second step advancing.

*Discovering, then, that here the upper vertical plane is the widest,
invites to read the figure downward which reverses
(a), (b), (c), (d) to 4 more different readings: (e), (f), (g), (h).*

Therefore, the small figure offers 8 different readings.   J. A.

12

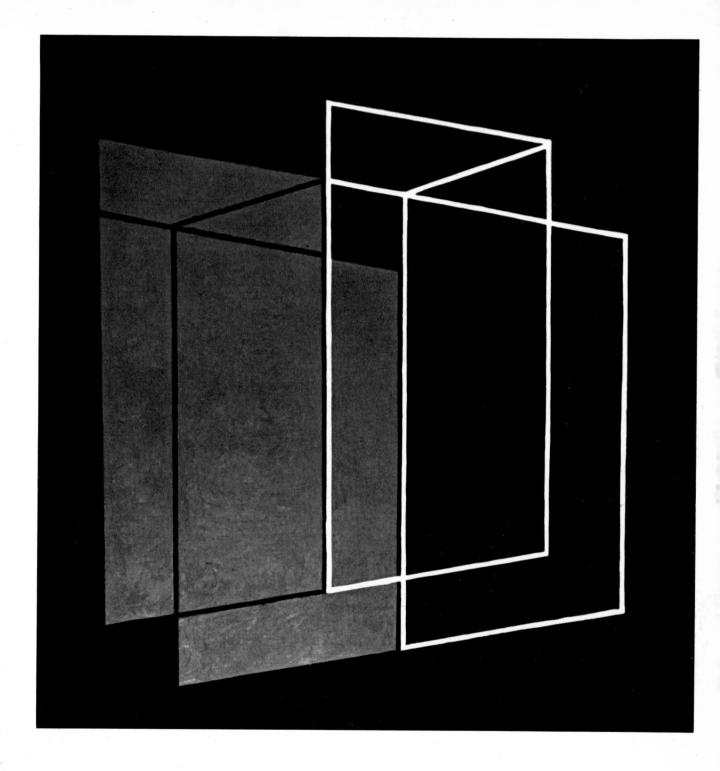

+ = −

The more
the sun shines,
the more
water evaporates,
clouds appear,
and the sun
– shines less.

The less
the sun shines,
the less
water evaporates,
clouds diminish,
and the sun
– shines more.

Da capo.

J. A.

Men of insight are brief. Whatever they create is of sparse complexity. On the surface it may seem obvious, so that the one who does not care to listen or to look will be satisfied and on his way. But the one whose eye is sharp will pierce surface vision. He will systematically explore the labyrinth which discipline built to channel human perception.

Such is the constructional work of Albers: Deceptively simple yet immensely sophisticated. It requires the spontaneous vision of a child or the eye of a traveller for whom the landscape changes with every step he takes or with every turn of the wheel.

A straight line as defined by geometry cannot appear in nature. Still we characterize the visible limit of an ocean plane, the steppe horizon, a shaft of light, or the meeting of crystalline surfaces as a straight line. The rarity of lines in nature points out a fundamental difference between art and the natural world. For art, even if it does imitate nature, is by necessity abstraction and therefore between the realm of geometry and the organic.

Man's early visual creations were linear experiments. Prehistoric painting and often very abstract popular art were mostly linear. Eventually the highly sophisticated and magical patterns of the Barbarian nations during the period of migration prove that line can become a primary artistic concern and an important step in the human ability of thought and abstraction.

One of the most moving observations to be made at Lascaux is to see that line as an expressive carrier of meaning, and abstract rectangular forms, that is, the appearance of geometry, are on the same walls. In this way the emergence of painting and geometric thought are inextricably connected.

With the origin of artistic activity the concept of bilateral symmetry is discovered as an ordering principle. A child circling an animal will observe that both its sides are similar. In primitive society the wish for a simultaneous totality leads to the creation of the double-headed totem. Albers experimented with the fact that, while rhythmically drawing, man's left hand will learn or imitate what his right hand is doing.

Lines and symmetry became the most frequently used formal conventions. To make them the basis of a sustained artistic statement betrays either a single-minded naïveté or a boldness of imagination in the attempt to create an original rearrangement of the obvious. This in turn requires a deep knowledge of our visual reactions.

Why, then, should Albers' constructions using the conventional produce unconventional results? Why should the seemingly cool intellectual approach not compare with geometric constructions or optical illusions, and produce an enduring and rich visual experience instead?

Following an exact drawing, Albers has white lines mechanically incised into the strongly contrasting black ground with utmost precision. Except for an increase or decrease in linear activity there is nothing else. This starkness demands a concentration of vision, forces us to continue our exploration or to give up, knowing that we have been superficial. Another difficulty lies in the fact that the eye in search of reality or perhaps ultimate truth, wants to see more than the artist expresses. But here through the excitement of the unresolvable it stays bound to the work of art and develops new techniques for seeing.

Visual tension is achieved through an occasional almost imperceptible deviation of diagonals and counter diagonals from the vertical or horizontal. Lines defining the composition are almost never parallel to the frame or sharp outer edge. The underlying checkerboard module of the whole construction is often shown through a thinly frosted area, while visual guide lines are thicker and provide carefully placed accents. Due to bilateral or even quadrilateral symmetry our eye begins to turn in a ceaseless exploratory process, starting and restarting from left or right, from top to bottom, and up again.

This ever changing viewpoint forced upon us transforms the position of each line in relation to the other in space. We begin to see structural planes moving in front of other planes which themselves, in a renewed visual exploration, will now seem behind the formations we first had visualized as being further removed. (See detailed description, p. 12.)

We begin to reconstruct seemingly fragmentary forms, trying to establish a relation to Euclidean geometry, but our unwarranted imposition is repeatedly and instantly destroyed by the motion of our eyes. Concavities become convexities, what was looked upon is now seen from below.

Thus the visual migration – guided by line chords and echoed by subdominant thinner lines – moves through a constant transformation of the easily recognizable theme and comes close to the musical experience of, for example, Bach's 'mirror pieces'. Both are full of startling surprises which are consciously as well as rhythmically enjoyed.

A hegemony of lines creates planes and finally ungraspable space. The inherently neutral straight line achieves a vivid interplay of surprising forms.

Art is not to be looked at – art is looking at us.   J. A.

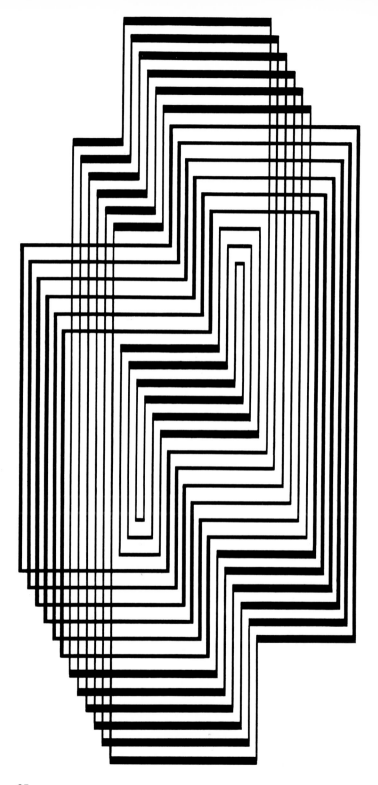

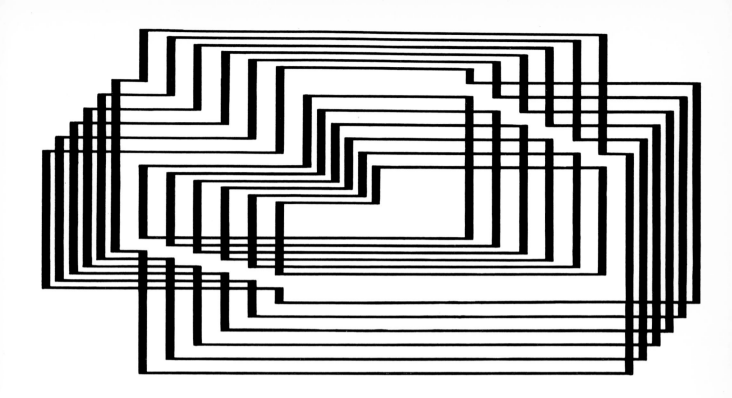

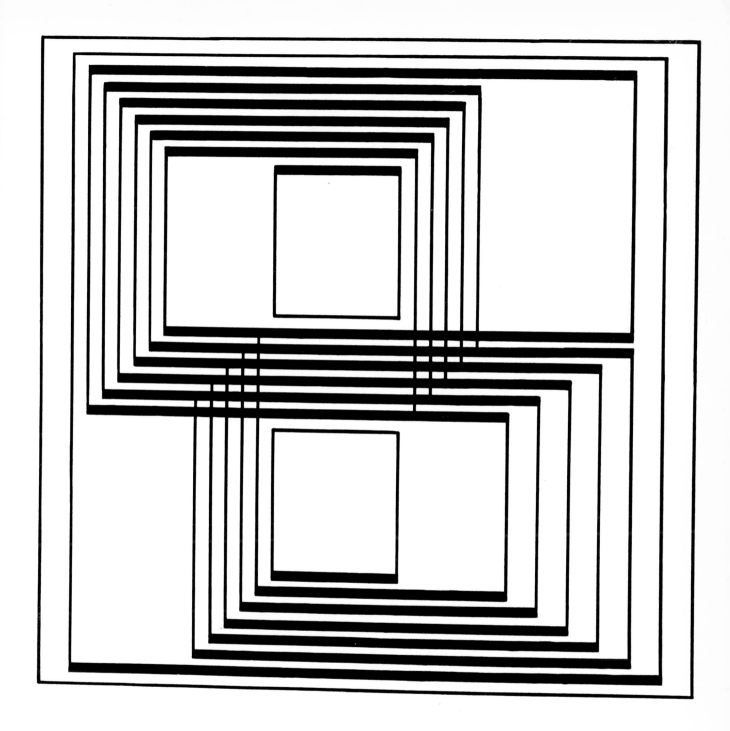

Geometric shapes compel certain emotional reactions because we interpret them through a projection of the energies acting upon our bodies. A rectangle on its long side will *rest*. *Standing* it will suggest vertical motion or at least have an upright impact. A triangle balanced on its point will give the impression of unstable equilibrium. The forms which Albers uses frequently possess a neutral Platonic perfection until they are set off against one another. Then they grow tense, lose their rational and static perfection, and become dynamic. Relative to one another they escape into irrational spatial systems until – held together by larger forms – they are compressed back into an ever-changing stability. Their stability is change.

In a series of statements, Albers characterized his 'Graphic-tectonic' lithographs as

stable yet dynamic,
flat yet deep,
uncolored yet colorful,
simple yet complex.

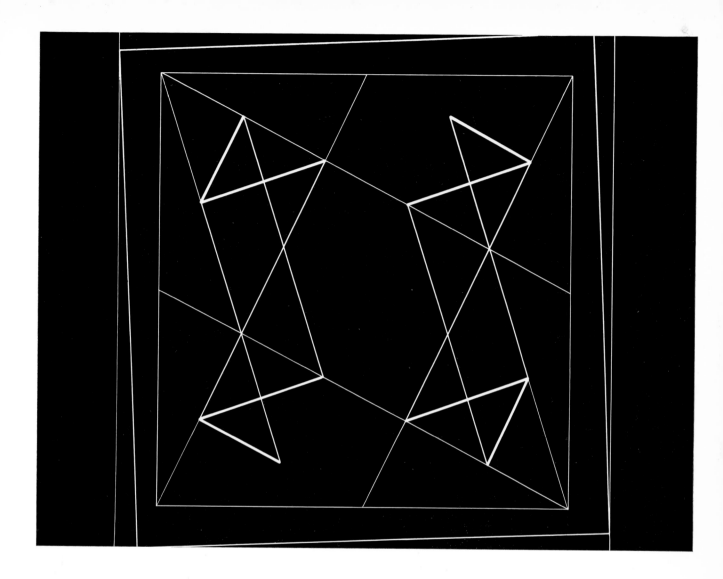

In the austere pictorial world of Albers everything becomes of equal importance. Forced to look closely, the observer is made aware of the fact that he usually tends to notice only those aspects of works of art which are important to him as an individual, and to neglect or ignore the rest.

There is no hierarchy of interest in Albers' work and only hints as to perceptual categories. Unaware, the viewer is guided towards total perception and away from preconception.

The flat plane consists, by definition, of the track left by a straight line in a sideway motion. Curved surfaces can be extremely complex and seem more interesting. Since Albers chose the straight line, he consistently represents the simplest two-dimensional form: a portion of a plane.

Once the observer has begun to organize the different connected planes which recede into illusory space, he must reorganize them to avoid their illogical twisting.

For Albers has achieved what few have seen and tested: planes can be made to twist controllably through their integration with two established space systems. The frothy, brittle texture of the planes enhances the impossibility of this bothersome twist until one learns to accept this unexpected mobility as yet another visual experience.

Furthermore, planes which seemed to support each other cannot structurally do so though they are visually held together. The composition finally becomes weightless as a thought.

Simple forms then reveal more facets and surprises than one has attributed to them. In this rich life of dematerialized form, the immediately visible world becomes one of the possible frames of reference.

This figure extends vertically – but also in the round –
between 2 equal figures (in heavier lines) at the top
and at the bottom, equal in form, size, and inclination,
though of reversed direction.

Each of the 2 figures consists of a longer middle line
from which 3 shorter parallel branch lines extend,
2 from the ends to the same side, and the third one
from the middle to the opposite side. As a result
of their reversed placement, the upper figure opens to the left
and upward, the lower one to the right and downward.

Thus, we see the whole in 2 ways: from above down
and, from the bottom upward. And the parallelogram
between the 2 middle lines appears – twisted.

The axis of this parallelogram connects in 2 right angles
the 2 middle branches. Their ends are connected
by 2 verticals, upward at the left, and downward at the right
with the opposite end branches. Thus they form
bilateral wings with bends of no ending. And,
in connection with the twisted parallelogram, they are
impossible to think or to see through.

Moreover, the 8 outer points of the 6 end branches
(including 2 pointed corners of the twisted parallelogram,
as well as the ends of the 2 bent wings) all are
imbedded in just 4 sides of a turned but frontal square
despite the fact that these 8 points exist in
4 different distances from us.

This is to show that such flexible relatedness is possible
only within the limitations of 2 dimensions,
that is, within an abstraction:
that 2 dimensions permit illusions, readings,
– impossible within the reality of 3 dimensions.   J. A.

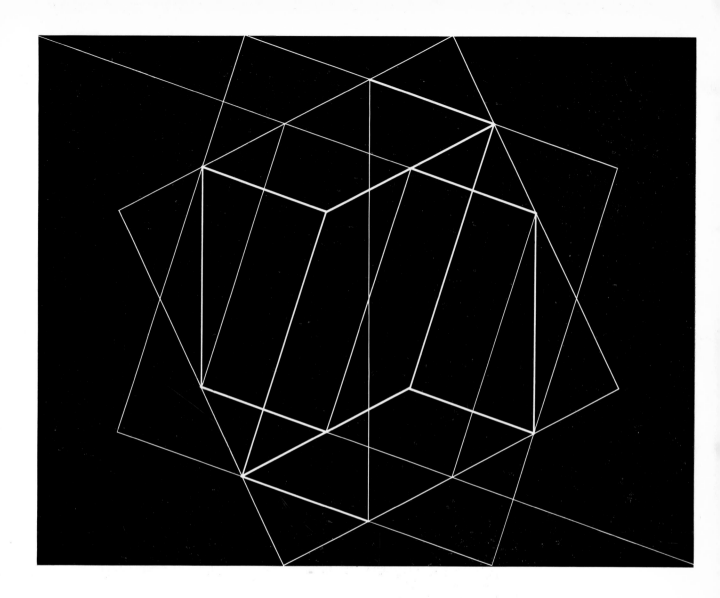

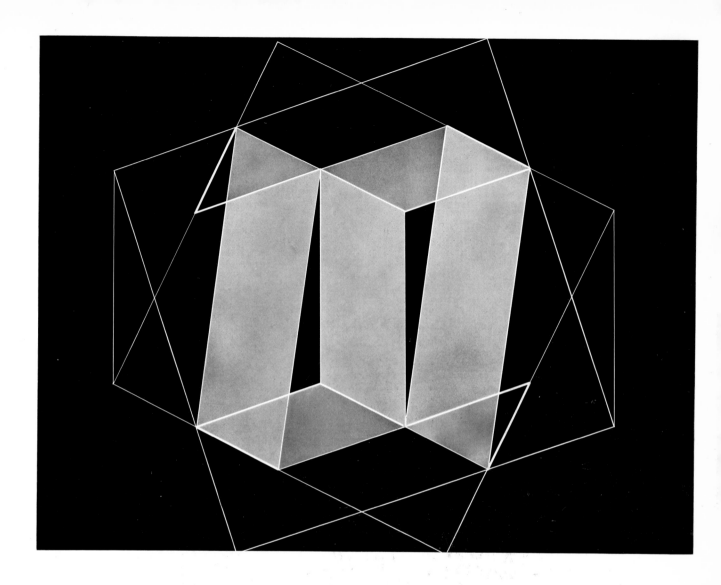

Apparently, it is little recognized that a right angle – 90° –
on a frontal plane is perceived – normally – as frontal,
which means flat, or full face, or 'en face' in French.

As this may seem to be a matter of course, let us remember
that most angles, acute or obtuse, are rarely seen as 2-dimensional
but from below, from above, or sideward, and, therefore, seen in
profile, and foreshortened, which really means – in 3 dimensions.

As a contrast, the 3 constituents of a right angle,
the vertex and the 2 legs, appear equidistant from the onlooker.
Therefore, we focus them within a frontal plane. And,
this remains – as a rule – independent of placement
and attitude, as well as of length of legs, equal or different.

In the accompanying construction, the 2 rectangles within the 2 figures
in heavier lines, surprise with a different behavior.
Comparing the 3 structural points of the rectangles, namely,
vertices and ends of the legs, as to their placement, we will notice
that they do not appear within the frontal projection plane.

The vertices, and, with them, the legs, appear as
bent forward, or lifted in direction toward us,
which presents an unusual position and a rare sight.

The same phenomenon can be seen in constructions C 1 and C 2.

J. A.

The 'leading voices' here are 2 gray parallelograms
of precisely the same shape, size, and position.
They also are placed at the same level as all corners
of one parallelogram correspond horizontally
with equal corners of the other.

This means, they are 'factually' – which is geometrically –
neither in front nor behind, neither above nor below each other,
as they 'actually' – which is visually – make us believe.

This is easier to perceive when we imagine that both
top and bottom edges were horizontal. Then
the lozenge shapes would become rectangles, and so
would be seen as frontal, and therefore, as equidistant.

The 2 accompanying figures in heavy lines
connected with, but also overlapping, the parallelograms,
and which may remind us of the capital letter K,
are also precisely alike, and equally placed.
They perform a similar illusion in motion and placement.

The slanting lines of the K start at the left verticals
of the parallelograms. They seem hinged to it
within a planary angle of 90°. Whereas the downward line
moves forward and lands in front of its parallelogram,
the upward line of the K performs 2 contradicting actions.

First – up to the crossing – it moves within the hinged 90° plane,
and thus forward. But then, suddenly, it bends –
in a backward leaning – into the diagonal of the parallelogram,
and so is alternating the K into a twisted X.

Such illusions of fore and back, of turning and bending,
mislead us to see the square which embraces the parallelograms
– as leaning backward – which present an unusual sight
to be explained in C4.

And the function of the remaining lines?
Besides working to bring about such illusions, they are to prove
that here neither directions nor points are arbitrary.

All lines move within only 4 directions.
All points are crossings of a checkerboard-like grill,
including the 4 corners of the background, that is,
the 4 corners of the stage of performance.   J.A.

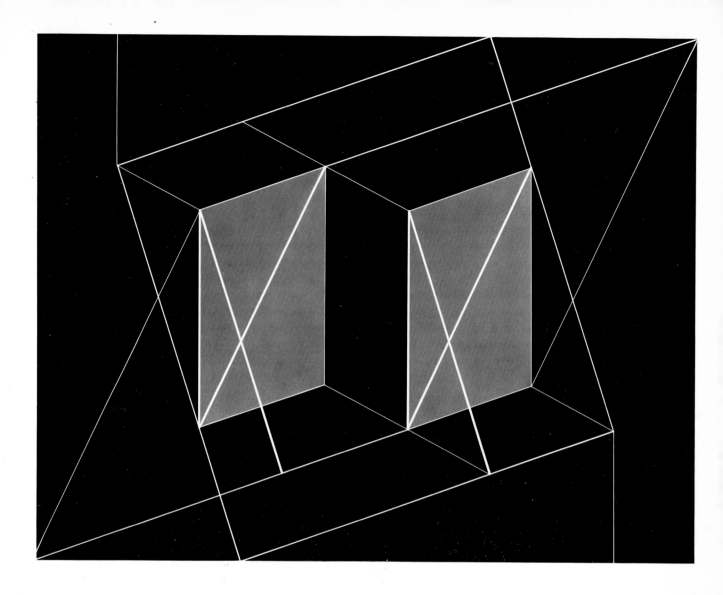

IV   Volumes and solids

Time used to move inexorably forward. Historical writing and memory are influenced by our knowledge of the final result of an event which retroactively influences our interpretation of a particular fact.

Thus the shadow of Waterloo hovers over Napoleon's coronation. Today we can resurrect objective and detailed fragments of the past through films and soundtrack. A moment of the past can be watched and heard as an unchangeable repeatable drama creating a future which is known, since for us it is also already past.

The difference between early and recent efforts to commit the past to the present is only gradual. We work against time in our discovery of forgotten cultures. Detached from the bridge of memory, these blocks of the past influence our period with incongruous immediacy.

Nineteenth century beliefs that it could be possible to record and measure all things in terms of time, space and pitch was, however, thoroughly shaken through the theory that, in space motion, time might be blotted out, at least in relation to earth hours. The stable pitch of sound is distorted in the Doppler effect.

Einstein stated that observers of atomic phenomena could no longer be objective, since their observations did not conform to fall into their usual pattern of experience of time and space, and thus could only interpret, but not describe, what they saw.

In spite of this new flexibility of formerly stable and safely established constants, the visual realm was little affected. The Cubists, as mentioned, tried to introduce a time element into their representation of solids through distortions. The Surrealists showed a series of arrested movements.

But the effect of multiple images experienced simultaneously in a group of objects could be produced in reality by mirrors or by stroboscopic photographs.

Albers is one of the few who has passionately analyzed the multiple polarity of bodies in time.

Instead of complex visual trickery, which was a plaything to many artists of the past, he uses the simple means of cool craftsmanship to turn and flatten 'solids', occasionally even breaking them up in a sequence of visual events.

Thus, in a constant test of our ignorance about the behavior of matter, one of the meanings of his works emerges from a negation of the inviolability of solids in time.

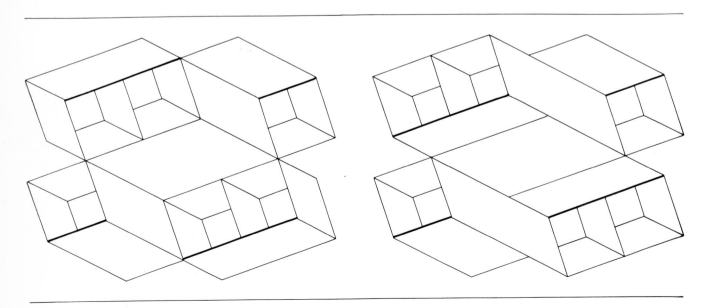

Volumes and solids are a primary tactile experience. A child touches before he sees. All objects within close enough visual range possess volume and weight.

Our judgment of the character of an object depends on our ability to focus on it. Since they elude sharp focus due to light refraction, it is difficult for a layman to estimate the value or even judge the authenticity of precious stones. Complex and rough textured materials or extremely simple geometric volumes appear to be heavier than their flat or curvilinear counterparts.

Albers reverses many of these primary processes in his representation of 'solids'. The lines delineating his volumes are sharp. The use of linear orthogonal perspective houses them in space. At the same time the large forms are often defined by parallels and become patterns which tend to merge with the pictorial surface. But then again the planes begin to escape our 'visual touch'.

Medieval and Byzantine space organization meets in the observer's eye, while Renaissance perspective relates the vanishing point directly to the limited human beam of vision. In both cases the infinite is made finite, space is related to man's reality, and each object has a fixed position.

It is interesting that Albers should choose a system of orthogonal perspective whose parallel lines go 'through' the viewer. Since their beginning or end is not attached to any frame of reference in our experience, the effect is one of dematerialization. This enables his volumes to be simultaneously aggressive and recessive. They play games with our eye muscles, which must be constantly on one object while the other slips away. Their clear structure is not related to any frame of reference. They have moved beyond the vanishing point where solids become flickering, immaterial constellations.

Their crystalline structure does not have any density. They possess an intellectual focus and an inner reality. In these solids which exert no pressure and which in their constant motion defy measurement, conflict and tension become pure form. Their mystical transformation is matter-of-fact and has nothing to do with ecstasy. The vision they produce is free of fakery and romanticism. It shares its deep concentration upon the reaction of the human eye with the experiments of early Renaissance painters who relentlessly searched for a system of spatial illusion. Like their work it is free of incidentals.

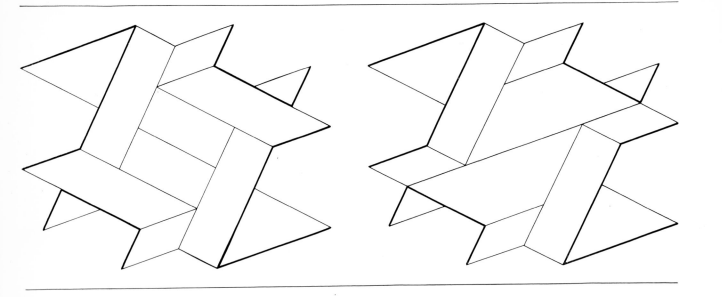

4 Pairs of Structural Constellations

Within a formal limitation of equal contours
as mutual silhouette, these pairs show different
but related plastic movements of lines, planes, volumes.

Thus, they change
in motion: from coming to going,
in extension: from inward to outward,
in grouping: from together to separated,
in volume: from full to empty,
or reversed.

And all this, in order to show extended flexibility.   *J. A.*

52

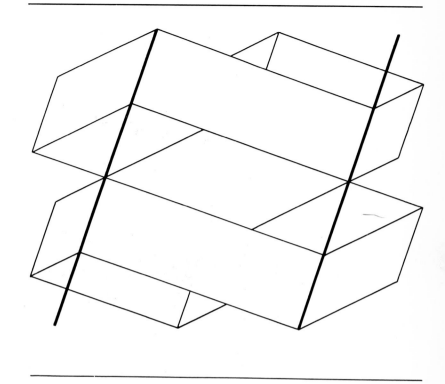

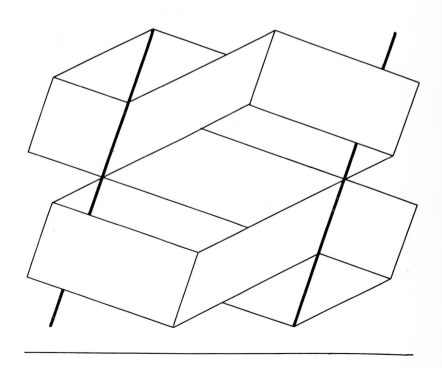

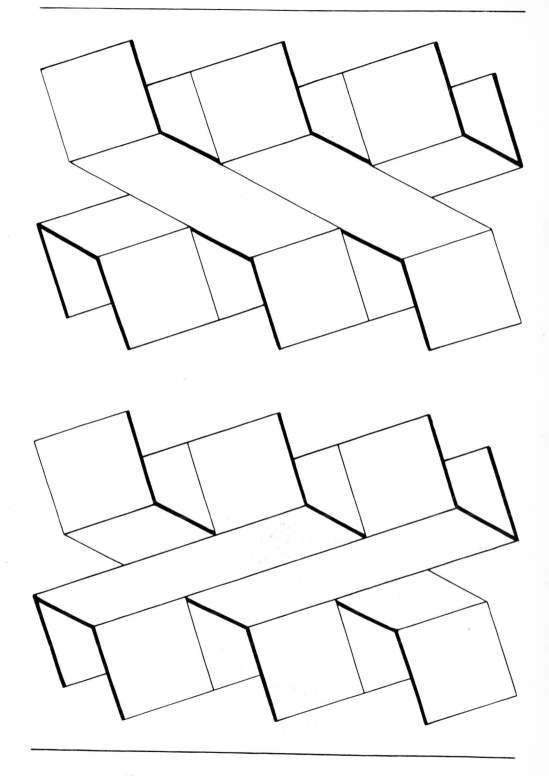

V Motion in time

Rapid motion within seemingly stable systems has changed our daily way of life as well as our inner imagery.

We sit in a car or in a plane while the landscape slips by. Rocks change their shape, rivers and roads change their course relative to our eyes. Façades rise while we approach, recede and decline while we go on. Matter, the matrix of being, has become a function of energy and its dynamic and infinite transformations.

This, then, is the world out of which the work of Albers grows and can present to us the relativity of our most basic experiences. Forced to test again and again all that we see, we learn to see more.

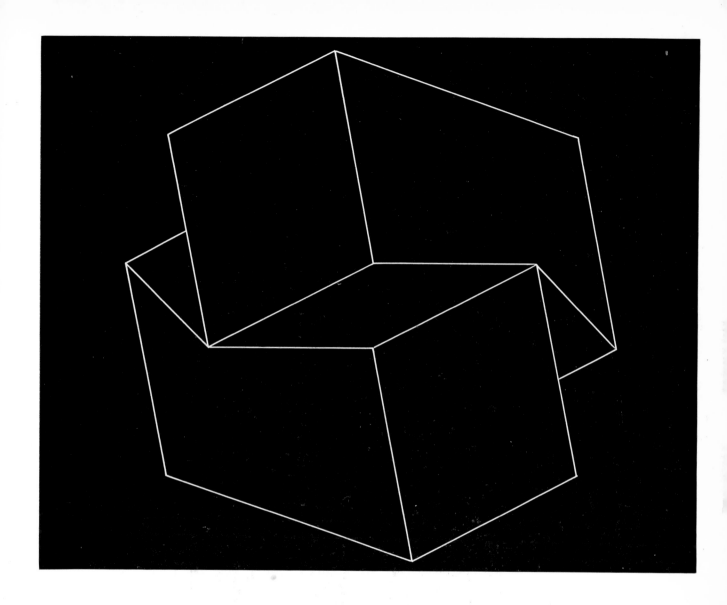

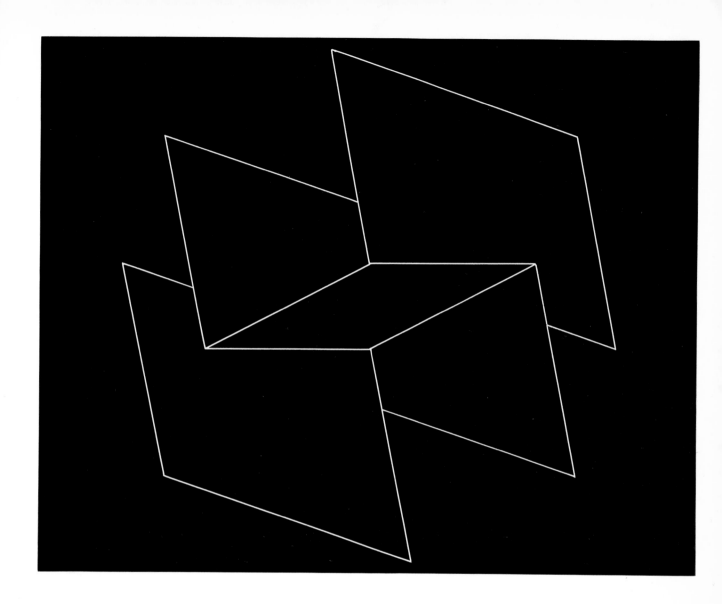

All art demonstrates
constant change
in seeing and feeling.   J. A.

Language can describe only the simplest forms of motion with precision: circular, elliptical, straight, zig-zagging. Complex movements are circumscribed: graceful, clumsy, tottering. Many of these descriptive terms are interchangeable: tottering, swaying. Since motion involves the change in position of a solid in space and time, that is, three things about which we know very little, it is natural that our words for it lack clarity.

Efforts to give an illusion of motion in painting achieved a magnificent climax in the spatial explosions of Baroque ceilings. But in these representations of a moment every point is fixed in space. In other words, a dramatic figural scene will show a series of single motions, based on lines which can be diagonals, spirals; and can as such recede, curve, or be in a simpler relationship in regard to the frame of the painting or its surface. Even a bent spiralling column can still be easy to represent. All these types of motion are self-contained, can be reproduced mechanically, and each part can be exactly located within a perspective grid system. They are part of a system which includes friction, leverage, weight, and counterweight.

Today our frame of reference and our geometries are changing. The crisp shaded planes which Albers uses are never at rest. They equivocally recede and advance while they turn. Lines meeting at a 90° angle bend forward and backward, remaining right angles. Statically, Albers had explored the color phenomenon of vibrating planes in his painting. In his graphic work vibration is transformed into a sequence of visual events caused by motion within the planes themselves and through space. The constantly changing relationships of shapes in space can only be seen in a time sequence. In the work of Albers, space and time are thus inextricably connected.

These experiments are probably his most important and as yet least developed discovery. They elegantly begin an honest visual exploration of little-known characteristics of non-Euclidian dimensions.

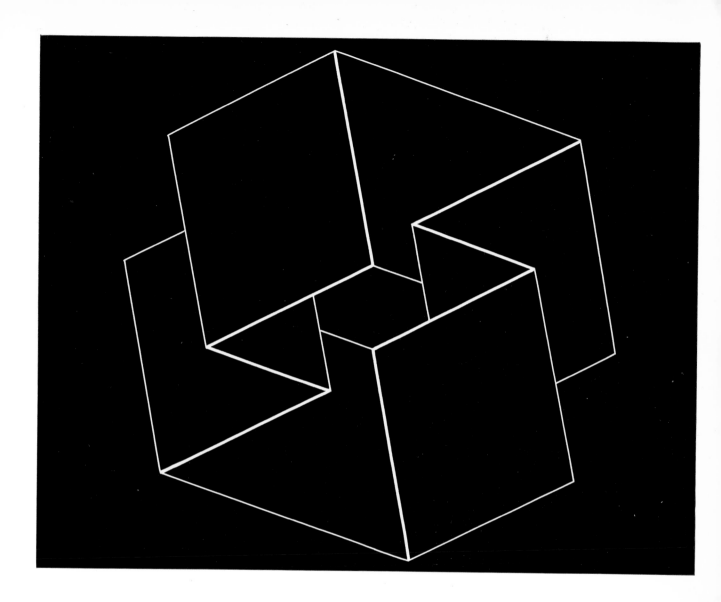

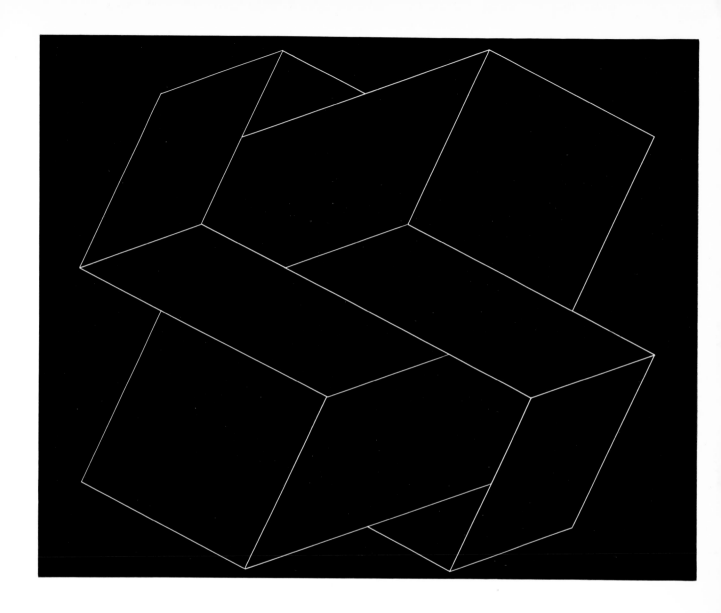

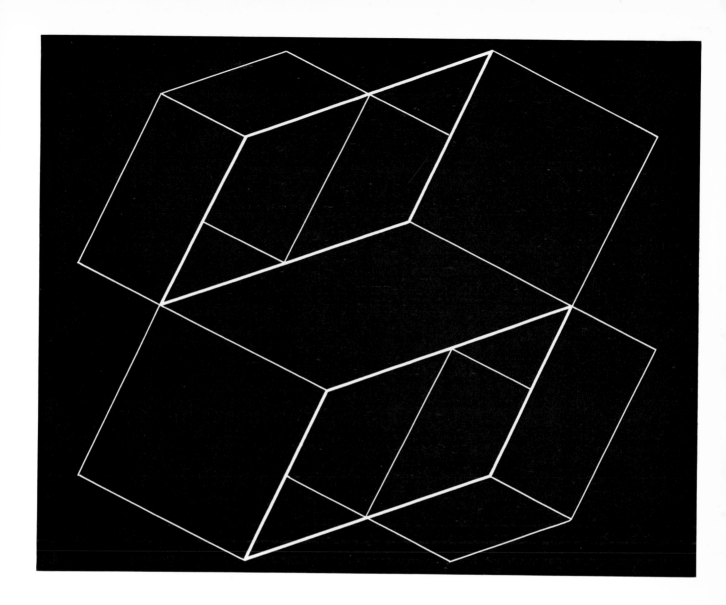

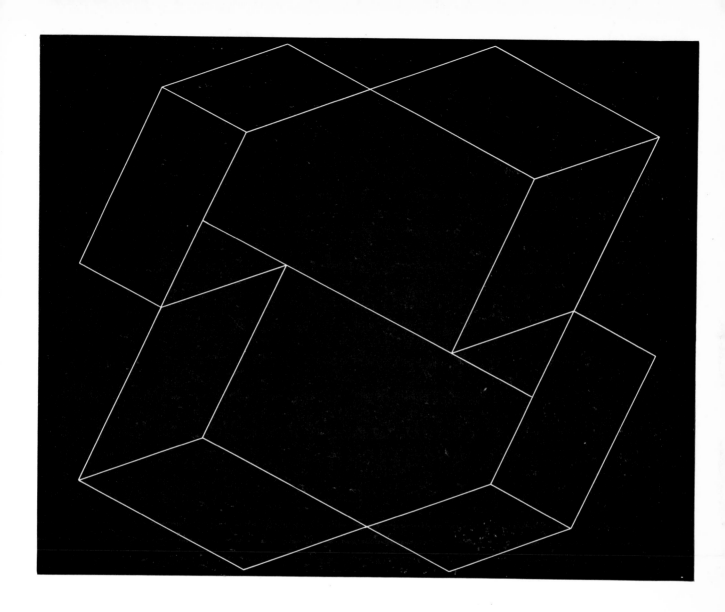

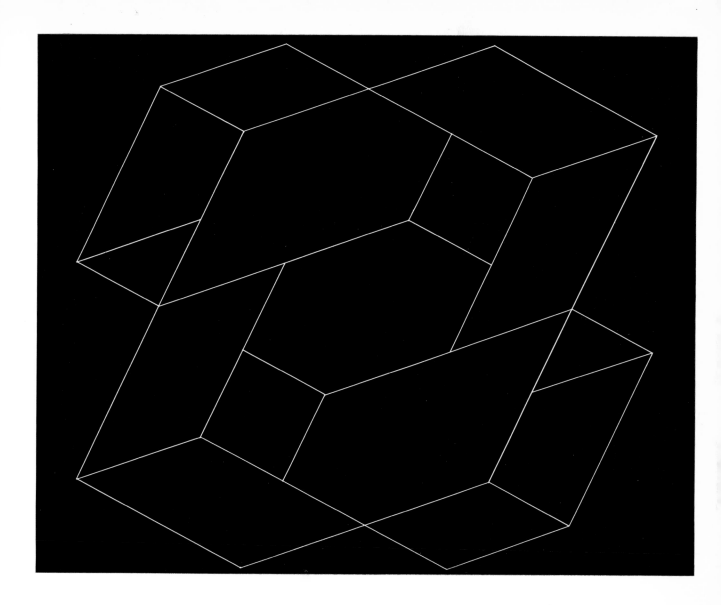

VI   Conclusions

The aim of life
is living creatures.
The aim of art
is living creations.

J.A.

These are the elements of Albers' constructed work:

His tools: A ruler, a pen, a checkerboard graph paper.

His means: The drawn or incised straight line forming patterns, volumes, or achieving motion, frequently organized so as to form a bilaterally reversible image and suspended within a neutral black or white ground.

His subject: Line creating a sequence of visual events in a purely pictorial space.

His aim: To shape new, valid visual systems based on the supremacy of line. To break down object reality, creation of a labile balance of form and unexpected mobility within constantly changing, easily readable configurations. To show unexpected weaknesses within visual conventions. Through concentration on a severe element – excluding all else – to force the observer to follow and to continue an endless experiment.

His result: Creation of an image detached from all literary allusion. Subject and object, confinement and infinity, material and immaterial, space and time, perception and concept, form a unity. Each work is its own frame of reference. Albers' prismatic world full of visual spectra contains slight but infinite variations, each of which is significant and provides the emotion of discovering a hitherto unknown element. Thus in a sequence of visual events delight is created. Albers' ceaseless investigation contributes a new diagram of reality to the art of the present.

To design is
to plan and to organize, to order, to relate and to control.
In short it embraces
all means opposing disorder and accident.
Therefore it signifies
a human need
and qualifies man's
thinking and doing.   J.A.

Anonymous, consciously limited art is unfashionable. Stripped of its creator and of a personal touch, the work of Albers forbids an easy familiarity. Often his plates or drawings are unsigned and exclude – as far as possible – superficial identification. Albers believes that 'somebody else' could create similar works. But few would have his mastery of restricted means and could as relentlessly as he reach out for a geometric dream.

In a way, his work possesses the severity of Classicism in its exclusion of incidentals and concentration on a compositional framework which will absolve man from imperfection and become part of an ideal realm. One might think of the impeccable peace in David's painting of the dead Marat. One might be reminded also of the concentration on a motive or object matter in the visual exercises which characterize American realism.

In these movements literary allusion is subjected to the strictest formal discipline. At the same time we think of Cubism and especially Constructivism and their early abstract theories. Even more basically the art of Albers finds its inspiration in the great decorative inventions which survived millenaries detached from time-bound individuals. Describing the meander, Albers mentions that 'such meaningful form has excited people for ages, all over the East–Western world from China–Japan to Greece, and particularly in the New World from the Tlingits, one of the most northern tribes, to the southern Araucanians.

But while these ornamental forms were in search of dynamically stable repetitive systems, Albers presents unique cases of consistently illogical occurences which belong to the realm of ever-changing forms of energy.

Art is to present
vision first,
not expression first.
Vision in art is to reveal
our insight – inner sight,
our seeing
the world and life.

Thus art is not	*an object*
but	*experience.*
To be able	*to perceive it*
we need to be	*receptive.*
Therefore art is	*there*
where art	*seizes us. J. A.*

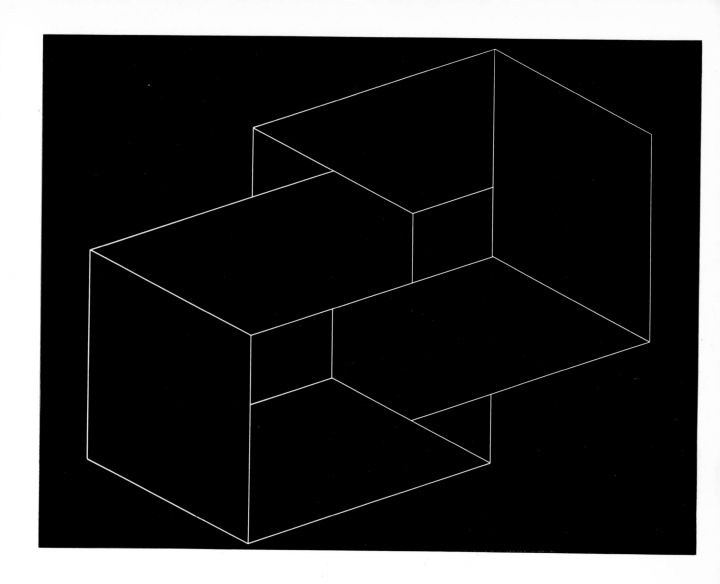

In this irrational interpenetration of 2 open cubes we notice
first the heavy top and bottom edges of the front openings.
They are presented by 4 lines equally long and thick,
and, as parallels, equally oblique.

Because of their equalness and their placement, they appear
as 2 pairs of lines of equal height and width.
Although staggered, geometrically they belong to 1 plane.

But soon it becomes dubious whether they are parallel.
It seems that they belong to a convex plane, or even
to a twisted plane. Convex, because the interiors
behind the openings converge. Twisted, because
the axes of the interiors are bent down at right, up at left.

And with this corresponds that we see the cubes
at right from below, at left from above.

But the fact remains: the 4 lines – – are parallel.   J.A.

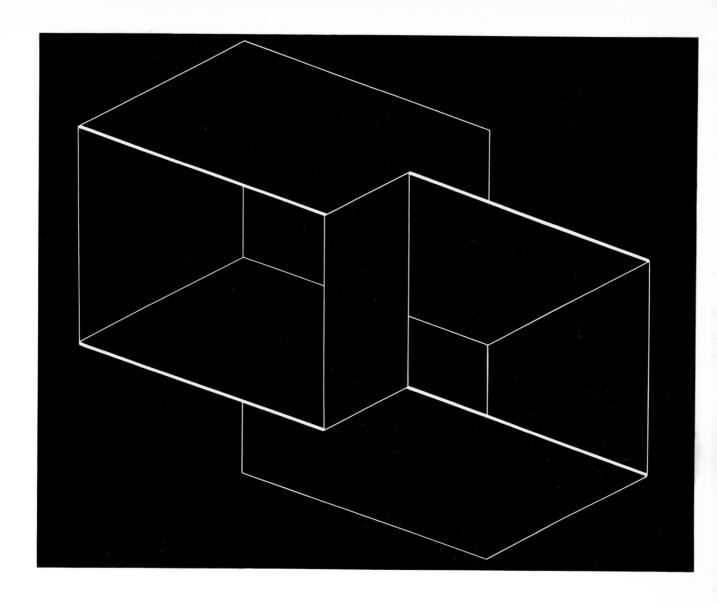

Through the exclusion of the obviously subjective and of any subject matter extraneous to the pictorial entity these parsimonious, severe constructions contain all Albers wants us to see within themselves. There is nothing outside the picture. It is autonomous, looks at its own changing physiognomy, and thus, in a way, is never alone. If man happens to look at it, it will change him.

Albers searches for visual truth, consistently transcending the obvious to explore delicate pictorial mechanism arrived at after long extensive experimentation, and comparing as many possibilities as occur.

Easy – to know
that diamonds – are precious.
Good – to learn
that rubies – have depth,
but more – to see
that pebbles – are miraculous.   J. A.

His model of the world is in eternal flux. 'Life is change', he wrote in 1935. He shows this ever-present change in its simplest, most uncompromising and basic form, and thus reiterates the attitude in Blake's symbolic statement that all infinity is contained in a grain of sand.

Through its simplicity, its order and control, and the subsequent resultant – untroubled freedom – the microcosm of Josef Albers ultimately disciplines change and thus denies chaos.

No time is – never
   never also everywhere
    everywhere is always
no time   *is always.   J. A.*

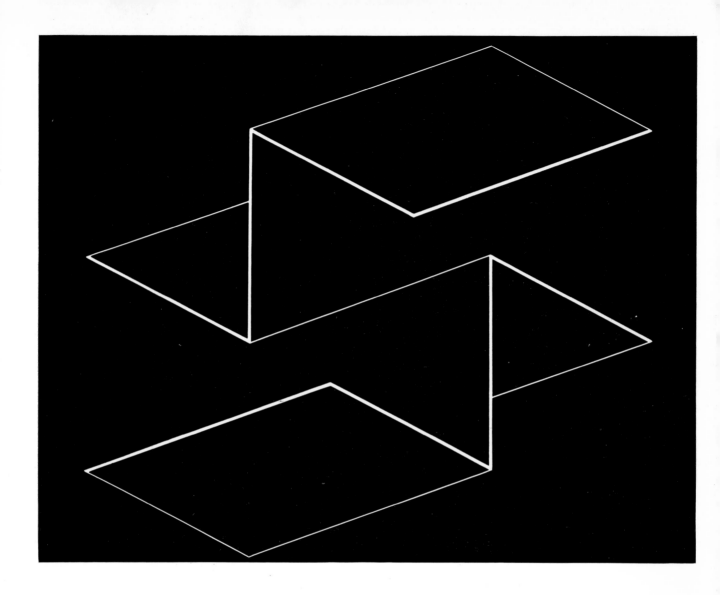

Biographical notes

Born   March 19, 1888, in Bottrop, Ruhr, Germany

Studied   Royal Art School, Berlin, 1913–1915
School of Applied Art, Essen, 1916–1919
Art Academy, Munich, 1919–1920
Bauhaus Weimar, 1920–1923

Taught   • Bauhaus Weimar – Dessau – Berlin, 1923–1933
• Black Mountain College, North Carolina, 1933–1949
Harvard University, Graduate School of Design, 1936, 1937
     Spring Semester 1941, Summers 1941 and 1950
Cincinnati Art Academy, 1949
Pratt Institute, Brooklyn, N.Y., 1950
• Yale University 1950–1960 (Chairman Art Department)
Havana University, 1952
Universidad Catolica, Santiago, Chile, 1953
Lima, Peru, School of Architecture, 1953
Ulm, Germany, Hochschule, 1953–1954, 1955
Honolulu University, Hawaii, Summer 1954
Syracuse University, N.Y., Summers 1958 and 1959
Carnegie Institute, Pittsburgh, 1957, 1958
Minneapolis, University, 1959
Kansas City Art Institute, 1959
Chicago Art Institute, 1959–1960
Atlanta Art Institute, Ga., 1960
Georgia Institute of Technology, Atlanta, 1960
Princeton University, 1960

Lives now in New Haven, Connecticut, USA

Selected bibliography

Only books or articles containing reproductions of the graphic construction by Albers are mentioned here.

G. H. Hamilton: Josef Albers. Paintings, Prints, Projects. (Catalogue for a retrospective exhibition. Excellent account including historical and bibliographical material.) Yale University Art Gallery, 1956.

Arts and Architecture, July 1947. Title page.

J. Albers: Present and/or Past. Design, April 1946.

Interior. Industrial Design, January 1947. Title page.

josef albers hans arp max bill. galerie herbert hermann, stuttgart 11, 1948.

Albers at the Cincinnati Art Museum, Cincinnati, 1949. Exhibition catalogue.

Time Magazine: Illustrated reports of Albers' exhibitions: January 1949, June 1956, January 1959.

Third National Print Annual Exhibition. The Brooklin Museum, March 1949.

News Bulletin. The Art Academy of Cincinnati, November 1949, vol. 1, No. 1.

Elaine de Kooning: Albers paints a picture. Art News, November 1950.

Contemporary Art Society, Cincinnati. Thirteenth Annual Interstate Exhibition, November 1951.

V. D. Lozza: Espacio y Tiempo in Perceptismo teorico y polemica, No. 5, 1952 (Buenos Aires).

Josef Albers. New Mexico Quarterly, University of New Mexico, Winter 1953.

El Arquitecto Peruano, Lima, September/October 1953.

Josef Albers on Art. One-quarter scale, University of Cincinnati, March 1953.

Josef Albers. Nueva Visión, No. 8, 1955, Buenos Aires, 21 illustrations, 1955. Exhibition catalogue.

J. Charlot: Nature and the Art of Josef Albers. College Art Journal, spring 1956.

J. McHale: Josef Albers. Architectural Design, London, June 1956, 15 illustrations.

M. Loew: Albers, impersonalization in perfected form. Art News, April 1956.

josef albers, fritz glarner, friedrich vordemberge-gildewart. kunst-
haus zürich, 28 april bis 10 juni 1956. Exhibition catalogue.

Josef Albers. Karl Ernst Osthaus Museum, Hagen, 1957. Exhibition
catalogue.

Albers. Galerie Denise René, Paris, 1957. Exhibition catalogue.

josef albers zum 70. geburtstag. ausstellung vom 16 märz bis 13 april
1958. kunstverein freiburg im breisgau. Ulm 1958. 12 illustrations.
biography.

josef albers. ausstellung 7–31 mai 1958, amerikahaus, berlin.

Josef Albers: Poems and Drawings. The Readymade Press, New
Haven, Connecticut 1958. Several poems from this book are quoted
here by permission of the editor.

The Lit's salute to Albers. Yale Literary Magazine, International edition, 1958.

josef albers. zeichnungen – drawings. New York and Berne 1959.

Josef Albers. Print, vol. III, No. 4, Woodstock, Vermont (no date).

Spirale. M. Wyss, editor. Bern (no date). Important illustration material.

Josef Albers. Yale Literary Magazine, New Haven, 1960.

Josef Albers: Poems and Drawings – Gedichte und Zeichnungen.
Second edition, George Wittenborn, Inc. New York 1961.

josef albers: stedelijk museum, amsterdam, holland, 10 maart–10 april
61, nr 265. Exhibition catalogue.

Will Grohmann: Josef Albers. museum journal, amsterdam, serie 6,
no 9/10, april–mei 1961.

stedelijk museum, amsterdam, exhibition 'bewogen beweging',
III 10–IV 17, 1961. Exhibition catalogue.

E. H. Gombrich: How to Read a Painting. Saturday Evening Post,
Philadelphia, July 29, 1961.

List of illustrations

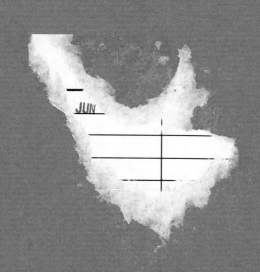
JUN